D1708153

RESCUE DOGS

by Kevin Blake

Consultant: Sue Kamell
President and Founder of Pet Rescue
Larchmont, New York

New York, New York

Credits

Cover and Title Page, © Alona Rjabceva/Shutterstock; Cover TR, © Kachalkina Veronika/Shutterstock; Cover CR, © Kevin Wolf/AP Images; Cover BR, © ncjMedia Ltd.; TOC, © tsik/Shutterstock; 4, © Scott Lehman/Shutterstock; 5T, © ncjMedia Ltd.; 5B, © Himagine/iStock; 6, © ncjMedia Ltd.; 7L, © ncjMedia Ltd.; 7R, © Francois Loubser/Shutterstock; 8, © hadkhanong/Shutterstock; 9, © Annette Shaff/Shutterstock; 10, © Kevin Wolf/AP Images; 11, © Stefano Tinti/Shutterstock; 12, © Straight 8 Photography/Shutterstock; 13T, © I-5 Publishing 2015; 13B, © Oksana Amelin/Dreamstime; 14, © Kachalkina Veronika/Shutterstock; 15T, © David Maialetti/Philly.com; 15B, © Leah-Anne Thompson/Shutterstock; 16, © New York State Police; 17, © bikeriderlondon/Shutterstock; 18, © Steve Meddle/Rex/REX USA; 19, © Mario Lopes/Shutterstock; 20, © SasPartout/Shutterstock; 21, © Steve Meddle/Rex/REX USA; 22, © Jerry Horbert/Shutterstock; 22B, © Gillian Laub; 23, © GlobalP/Thinkstock; 24, © Gillian Laub; 25, © The Washington Times/Zuma/Press/Newscom; 26, © Courtesy of Luciano Anastasini; 27, © Rick Purdue; 28, © Sue McDonald/Shutterstock; 29TL, © Nathan clifford/Shutterstock; 29TR, © dezi/Shutterstock; 29BL, © Eric Isselee/Shutterstock; 29BR, © Ermolaev Alexander/Shutterstock.

Publisher: Kenn Goin
Editorial Director: Natalie Lunis
Senior Editor: Joyce Tavolacci
Creative Director: Spencer Brinker
Design: Dawn Beard Creative
Photo Researcher: We Research Pictures, Inc.

Library of Congress Cataloging-in-Publication Data

Blake, Kevin, 1978- author.
  Rescue dogs / by Kevin Blake.
     pages cm. — (Dog heroes)
  Audience: Ages 7–12
  Includes bibliographical references and index.
  ISBN 978-1-62724-861-7 (library binding) — ISBN 1-62724-861-7 (library binding)
  1. Rescue dogs—Juvenile literature. I. Title. II. Series: Dog heroes.
  SF428.55.B53 2016
  636.7'0886—dc23
                              2015008106

For more information, write to Bearport Publishing Company, Inc., 45 West 21st Street, Suite 3B, New York, New York 10010. Printed in the United States of America.

10 9 8 7 6 5 4 3 2 1

Table of Contents

Fire!   4

Uno Saves the Day   6

Millions of Unos   8

People to the Rescue   10

Heroes for Heroes   12

Rescue Dogs on Patrol   14

Top Cop   16

A Rescue to the Rescue   18

Saved Again   20

A Second Chance   22

Pound Puppies   24

Showtime!   26

Just the Facts   28

Common Breeds:
    Rescue Dogs   29

Glossary   30

Bibliography   31

Read More   31

Learn More Online   31

Index   32

About the Author   32

Fire!

In 2014, on a warm summer night in Newcastle, England, Clare Whiteford and her three young sons were asleep on the second floor of their home. Without warning, a fire sparked downstairs in their kitchen. Orange flames and gray smoke soon spread throughout the room. Everyone in the family was unaware of the terrible danger—everyone except a five-year-old greyhound named Uno.

The smoke alarms in the Whiteford's house did not go off after the fire started.

Uno sprang into action. He raced upstairs to Clare's bedroom and barked loudly at her door. Clare heard Uno and followed the dog downstairs to the kitchen. Spotting the fire, she immediately rushed Uno and her children outside to safety and called for help.

Clare Whiteford and Uno

Greyhounds are tall dogs with long, powerful legs. At top speeds, they can run 43 miles per hour (69 kph).

Uno Saves the Day

Firefighters sped to the Whiteford home to put out the flames. After they **extinguished** the blaze, the firefighters told Clare what she already knew: Uno had saved their lives. If the greyhound hadn't woken her, the Whitefords might have been hurt or even died in the fire. "I've just no words to describe how I feel. He is our hero," said Clare.

The Whiteford family with their hero

Amazingly, just a year earlier, Uno didn't have a home. He had been used as a racing dog and then **abandoned** in a **shelter**. The Whiteford family had visited the shelter and **adopted** the big, lovable greyhound. So, before Uno rescued the Whiteford family, they had rescued him!

Because greyhounds are so fast, they are the **breed** most often used for racing. When greyhounds stop winning races or are too old to race, their owners sometimes abandon them or give them away.

After the fire, Uno received a trophy for his bravery.

Millions of Unos

There are millions of homeless dogs in the United States. The dogs are homeless for different reasons. Some are born without homes. Others are given up by their owners. Sometimes, dogs run away from home and then become lost. Sadly, other dogs are **abused** or **neglected** and must be taken away from their owners.

Many homeless dogs live on the streets, sometimes finding their food in trashcans.

Because there is such a large number of homeless animals, many dogs that are not adopted are "put to sleep," or **euthanized**. Some shelters, however, are "no-kill" and do no euthanize unwanted animals.

Many dogs that are homeless end up in shelters. Once there, they are given food and water. Some shelters with enough space are able to give the dogs a comfortable place to sleep and exercise. Shelter workers then try to find new homes for the dogs.

Many dogs in shelters are pit bulls. Pit bulls have a reputation for being dangerous, but if trained well, they often make great pets.

People to the Rescue

Beside shelters, there are many other organizations that help homeless dogs. Some organizations rescue any kind of dog. Others focus on certain breeds. For example, the National Greyhound Adoption Program (NGAP) finds loving homes for greyhounds like Uno.

Animal Rescue Team

humanesociety.org

A rescue worker helping a homeless mixed-breed dog

NGAP works hard to save unwanted greyhounds. **Volunteers** pick up homeless dogs and bring them to a special **kennel**. **Veterinarians** check and treat them for any injuries or illnesses. Then NGAP finds each dog a good home—saving thousands of greyhounds every year!

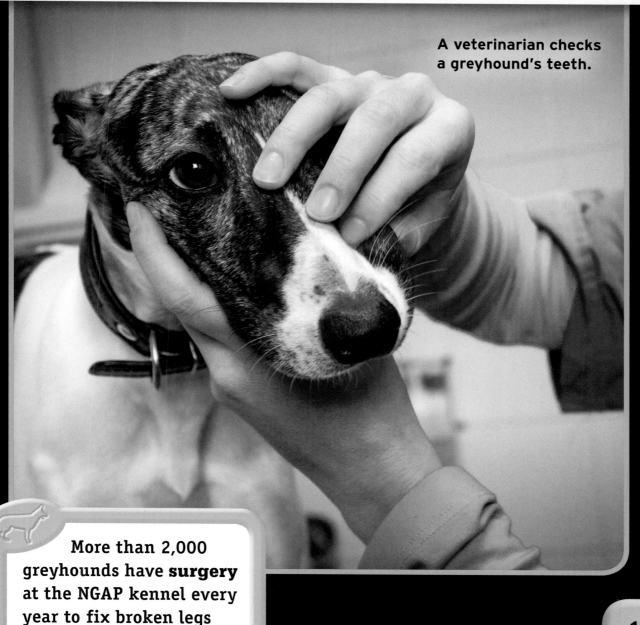

A veterinarian checks a greyhound's teeth.

More than 2,000 greyhounds have **surgery** at the NGAP kennel every year to fix broken legs and other racing injuries.

Heroes for Heroes

Other rescue organizations match homeless dogs with people who have special needs. **Veteran** José Pila came home from war suffering from nightmares and feeling **anxious** in crowds. A group called Pets for Vets paired José with a large, calm rescue dog named Ranger.

A veteran cuddles with a bulldog.

Ranger sleeps in José's bed and comforts him when he has a nightmare. The husky mix also helps José feel safe in large groups by walking close to his side. José has given Ranger a home—and Ranger has given José all the support and love he could have asked for.

José stands with his dog, Ranger. José has post-traumatic stress disorder, or (PTSD). PTSD is an illness that can make someone feel very sad or afraid.

Pets for Vets trains their rescue dogs to help veterans with special needs. Some dogs assist veterans in wheelchairs. Others simply provide love, comfort, and **companionship**.

Rescue Dogs on Patrol

Some rescue dogs help people by fighting crime. In Philadelphia, an organization called the Throw Away Dogs Project finds homeless dogs and trains them to be police dogs. The organization looks for canines that are playful and extremely energetic. "High-strung, for us, is a positive," says police officer and co-founder Jason Walters.

Many of the dogs in the program are German shepherds. Because they are intelligent, strong, and loyal, German shepherds often make great police dogs.

A German shepherd at a shelter

Once chosen, the dogs are sent to a special school where they are taught how to find criminals or missing people. Some dogs are also taught to sniff out drugs or bombs. Because the dogs are so energetic, they learn fast and don't give up easily. "Training these dogs is like playtime for them—their work is hide-and-seek," says Officer Walters.

Officer Jason Walters with his rescue dog, Winchester

This dog is being trained to use its sense of smell to find drugs or bombs.

Top Cop

In 2003, Wheeler, a German shepherd, was found wandering the streets of Brooklyn, New York. When **animal control** workers spotted him, he was starving and exhausted. They caught Wheeler and brought him to a city shelter. Luckily, an animal rescuer named Liz Keller spotted him there. Liz, who runs a rescue center in upstate New York, noticed he was energetic, intelligent, and protective. He had all the **traits** of a perfect police dog!

Wheeler poses for a picture

Liz donated Wheeler to the New York State Police. He attended a 20-week training program for police dogs in upstate New York. There, he learned how to use his excellent sense of smell to sniff out drugs and find missing people. After finishing the program, Wheeler became a member of the New York State Police. Since joining the police, Wheeler has found eight missing people and even tracked down a criminal hiding in the woods!

In 2014, there were more than 80 dogs working for the New York State Police.

A police dog sniffs a bag for drugs.

A Rescue to the Rescue

Rescue dogs don't need to have police badges to save lives. Some dogs, like Sheeba, help their owners live with deadly diseases. Sheeba's owner, Sara Russell, has a disease called **epilepsy.** This disease can cause Sara to have **seizures** and pass out.

Sara adopted Sheeba from a shelter near her home in England. Sheeba was a stray before shelter workers found her.

Sheeba is a German shepherd mix. Unlike most **service dogs,** she never received any training in how to help her owner.

One sunny afternoon, Sara took Sheeba for a walk. While crossing the road, Sara had a seizure and fell **unconscious** in the middle of the street. Just then, a car came speeding toward them. Using all of her strength, the brave dog dragged Sara to the side of the road right before the car zoomed by.

After Sara passed out, Sheeba had only seconds to save her life.

Saved Again

Saving Sara from being hit by a car was just one of Sheeba's heroic acts. Sheeba also came to her owner's aid when Sara had a seizure in the bathtub. After falling unconscious, Sara was in danger of slipping under the water and drowning. Once again, Sheeba sensed that her owner was in trouble and took action.

Sara can have a seizure at any time—even while taking a bath.

Sheeba jumped into the bathtub. Then she dragged Sara's body out of the water. When Sara finally woke up, she was lying on the bathroom floor. "Without Sheeba, I wouldn't be here today. She's a lifesaver," said Sara.

Some dogs can sense when their owner is going to have a seizure before it happens. Experts think they do this by picking up on small changes in the person's behavior or body temperature.

Sara's lifesaver, Sheeba

A Second Chance

In what other ways do rescue dogs make a difference in people's lives? They simply spread joy. That's what Luciano Anastasini does with his Pound Puppies circus act.

Luciano
Anastasini

Luciano and the Pound Puppies travel all across the country. They perform under a huge circus tent.

Luciano thought his work as a circus performer was over when he fell 50 feet (15 m) from a **high wire** and broke several bones. He knew he could never walk the high wire again, but he realized he could perform in a different way—with rescue dogs! He remembers thinking, "I'll give them a second chance. A purpose. Maybe it'll be my second chance." So Luciano visited shelters, searching for the perfect dogs to join his new circus team.

Luciano visited many shelters, like this one, looking for dogs.

Pound Puppies

Luciano found and trained dogs that no one else wanted. His first rescue was a beagle mix named Bowser, who was smart and could jump high. Luciano knew he could easily teach Bowser to jump over barrels and through hoops. Not long after, he spotted Penny, a fluffy white dog with a big grin.

Luciano holding Bowser

Penny had been abandoned because she spun around in circles and ran into walls. Luciano discovered that Penny walked this way because she is **cross-eyed**. He taught Penny to walk in a straight line by giving her treats. "She caught on fast," remembers Luciano. Before long, Luciano had put together a team of performing rescue dogs that included Bowser and Penny.

Penny (left) is a type of dog called a Bichon Frise.

Three different families had adopted Penny from the shelter and then returned her before Luciano found her.

Showtime!

When it's time to perform, Luciano and the Pound Puppies enter the circus tent on a tiny train. The dogs wait for Luciano's **commands**. Then they jump off the train, race up and down ramps, and sail through hoops. Some stand on their hind legs and dance. Others jump over Luciano as he somersaults.

Luciano and his dogs riding the train

Luciano performs with up to 15 dogs at one time.

Luciano's faith in these once-forgotten dogs has been met with cheering audiences. Fans love to watch the dogs do tricks and clown around. "A little love goes a long way with a dog," says Luciano.

The Pound Puppies draw cheers wherever they go.

Just the Facts

- More than one million dogs are rescued each year from shelters in the United States.

- Scientists have shown that people with dogs often have less stress and lower **blood pressure** than other people.

- Many people want to adopt puppies, leaving older dogs in shelters. However, older dogs are usually already house-trained and make wonderful pets.

- One of the largest no-kill animal shelters in the country is Best Friends Animal Society.

RESCUE DOGS

Any kind of dog, including purebreds and mixed breeds, can end up in a shelter and need to be rescued.

Greyhound

Pit bull

German shepherd

Mixed breed

abandoned (uh-BAN-duhnd) left alone and uncared for

abused (uh-BYOOZD) treated badly

adopted (uh-DOPT-id) taken in as part of a family

animal control (AN-uh-muhl kuhn-TROHL) a government group that manages stray pets and wild animals that wander into neighborhoods or towns

anxious (ANGK-shuhss) worried

blood pressure (BLUHD PRESH-ur) a measurement of the health of the heart and circulatory system

breed (BREED) a kind of dog

commands (kuh-MANDS) orders to do certain things

companionship (kuhm-PAN-yuhn-ship) providing company and friendship

cross-eyed (KRAWSS-eyed) having eyes that turn inward

epilepsy (EP-uh-*lep*-see) a brain disease that can cause seizures

euthanized (YOO-thuh-nyezd) when a sick or unwanted animal is killed

extinguished (ek-STING-gwisht) put out a fire

high wire (HYE WYE-ur) a thin wire set dangerously high in the air that a circus performer walks across

kennel (KEN-uhl) a place where dogs are raised, trained, or looked after

neglected (ni-GLEKT-id) not taken care of

seizures (SEE-zhurs) sudden attacks that can cause a person to shake and even lose consciousness

service dogs (SUR-viss DAWGS) dogs that are trained to do tasks for people who have disabilities or health problems

shelter (SHEL-tur) a place where homeless animals can stay

surgery (SUR-jur-ee) an operation that treats injuries or diseases by fixing or removing body parts

traits (TRAYTS) qualities or characteristics of a living thing

unconscious (uhn-KON-shuhss) not able to see, feel, or think

veteran (VET-ur-uhn) a person who has served in the armed forces

veterinarians (*vet*-ur-uh-NER-ee-uhnz) doctors who care for animals

volunteers (*vol*-uhn-TIHRZ) people who work without pay

Bibliography

Anastasini, Luciano. "Having Faith in Misfit Mutts." *Guideposts* (accessed on April 30, 2015).

Kehret, Peg. *Shelter Dogs: Amazing Stories of Adopted Strays.* Park Ridge, IL: Albert Whitman (1999).

Sacks, Amy. "Former Shelter Dog Fights Crime as Skilled Cadaver Dog." *New York Daily News* (February 24, 2012).

Read More

Fetty, Margaret. *Seizure-Alert Dogs (Dog Heroes).* New York: Bearport (2010).

Goldish, Meish. *Shelter Dogs (Dog Heroes).* New York: Bearport (2014).

Tagliaferro, Linda. *Service Dogs (Dog Heroes).* New York: Bearport (2005).

Learn More Online

Visit these Web sites to learn more about rescue dogs:

www.aspca.org

www.bestfriends.org

www.ngap.org

www.ny-petrescue.org

www.pets-for-vets.com

Index

Anastasini, Luciano 22–23, 24–25, 26–27

Bichon Frise 25
Bowser 24
Brooklyn, New York 16

epilepsy 18
euthanasia 8

German shepherds 14–15, 16–17, 18, 29
greyhounds 4–5, 6–7, 10–11, 29

Keller, Liz 16–17

National Greyhound Adoption Program (NGAP) 10–11
Newcastle, England 4
New York State Police 17

Penny 24–25
Pets for Vets 12–13
Philadelphia, Pennsylvania 14
Pila, José 12–13

pit bulls 9, 29
police dogs 14–15, 16–17
Post-Traumatic Stress Disorder (PTSD) 13
Pound Puppies 22–23, 24–25, 26–27

Ranger 12–13
Russell, Sara 18–19, 20–21

service dog 18
Sheeba 18–19, 20–21
shelters 7, 8–9, 10, 14, 16, 18, 23, 25, 28–29

Throw Away Dogs Project 14–15

Uno 4–5, 6–7, 10

veterans 12–13
veterinarians 7, 11

Walters, Jason 14–15
Wheeler 16–17
Whiteford, Clare 4–5, 6–7

About the Author

Kevin Blake lives in Providence, Rhode Island, with his wife, Melissa, and son, Sam. This is his seventh book for kids.